Country Living Collectibles
Rabbits

Country Living Collectibles

Rabbits

JESSIE WALKER

Hearst Books
New York

Country Living Staff

Rachel Newman, editor-in-chief

LIBRARY OF CONGRESS CATALOGING-IN-PUBLICATION DATA

Rabbits / by Jessie Walker.

      p.   cm.

ISBN 0-688-13100-X

1. Rabbits—Collectibles. I. Walker, Jessie. II. Country living (New York, N.Y.) III. Title: Country living collectibles

NK8608.R23 1996 745—dc20   96-1160

CIP

Printed in the United States of America

FIRST EDITION

1 2 3 4 5 6 7 8 9 10

BOOK DESIGN BY FLY PRODUCTIONS

Foreword

Several years ago, as photographer Jessie Walker and I approached Enid Hubbard's home in Northern California, we saw an idyllic portrait — a woman in a wide-brimmed garden hat cutting flowers in her front yard. Little did we realize that we were entering a world of fantasy and make-believe we would never forget. ❡ As Enid ushered us into her home, we were immediately greeted by rabbits — hundreds and hundreds of rabbits. We soon learned that they formed a collection of papier-mâché candy containers; all had been crafted in Germany. They were so lifelike in their poses and details, and they exuded such charm, I

felt that simply to document them in that house would not do justice to the collection as a whole, so Enid, Jessie, and I decided to create a book devoted to Enid's rabbits. ❡ In my eighteen years as editor-in-chief of Country Living, I had seen and photographed thousands of collections, from pull toys to potato mashers, but I had never come across a collection of such magnitude in one place. And I had never seen a collection of rabbits. I, like many of you, understand the collector's passion, so it is with great pleasure that I share this extraordinary warren of rabbits with you.

— RACHEL NEWMAN

Contents

Introduction

After photographing homes for Country Living *for more than eighteen years, I find the ones* that remain the most vivid in my memory are those enriched by collections that have been lovingly assembled by their owners. The collection might be of graphically designed, meticulously stitched Amish quilts from Pennsylvania or Ohio; fancifully painted pottery from the oceanside village of Quimper in Brittany, France; penny rugs crafted from circles of felt; or primitive game boards. Whatever form the collection takes, it imbues its owner's home

with a unique atmosphere and personality. ¶Of all the locations I have photographed over the years, none has delighted me as much as Enid and Tom Hubbard's stunning European country-style Northern California home with its bountiful accumulation of German papier-mâché candy-container rabbits — over a thousand of them — dating from the Victorian era. Some are realistic, replicating the woodland rabbits from the region of Thuringia where they were made. Some pull carts or stride about like miniature ponies, ridden by even smaller dolls. Many are dressed in period clothing and are happily engaged in a variety of human activities — primping in front of a mirror, pushing a wheelbarrow, or about to play tennis. ❡ These rabbits possess endearing, idiosyncratic characteristics, qualities of the individual as explained in one of my favorite quotations from the American philosopher William James: ❡ "In every concrete individual there is a uniqueness that defies all formulation. We can feel the touch of it and recognize its taste, so to speak, relishing or disliking, as the case may be, but we can give no ultimate account of it, and we have in the end simply to admire the creator." ❡ Enid's collection and the Hubbard pair of live Netherlands spot rabbits, Buttons and Bows, who inhabit a side-yard hutch designed as a miniature house, remind me of the love my sister and I shared for our own bunnies when we were children growing up in Wisconsin. Each day after school we would play with our beloved chinchillas, Flopsy and Mopsy, imagining them wearing Peter Rabbit jackets with large brass buttons and clog-type shoes as they bounded around our back yard. We also shared wind-up toys; one of our favorites was a bunny that hopped across the room, spitting out a piece of candy with each hop. ❡ Spending time with the Hubbard family and with Enid's collection, I understood how their whimsical and charming bunnies captured their hearts. They captured mine too.

The Roots of a Collection

Collections have a way of finding their collectors. This was the case with Enid Hubbard. Enid began her extraordinary collection of antique rabbit-shaped candy containers in 1981 when she discovered a small papier-mâché bunny "hopping" amongst pieces of majolica, the fanciful pottery she was then collecting. She hadn't the slightest intention of starting another collection. ¶ The sweet expression of that finely molded bunny, however, caught her eye and captivated her heart. She became smitten and began seeking out rabbits on all her shopping forays and antiquing trips. Over the years, as her rabbits began to multiply (as rabbits will), Enid came to appreciate the importance of putting together a collection that would be worthy of saving for future generations. Indeed, she plans to open a museum someday to exhibit her collection. ¶ Like all significant collections, Enid's rabbits bring together works of artistic merit, fine craftsmanship, and historic import. Candy containers were produced by the thousands in Germany for export to the United States from the Victorian age until the onset of World War II. After the Second World War, plastics *and other materials replaced papier-mâché and the quality of rabbits deteriorated. By the 1960s they were no longer made. ¶Many rabbits were given human attire and were anthropomorphized with the addition of human hands and feet. Many, too, were engaged in human activities. It is this crossover from animal to human that first enchanted Enid and then engaged her. If the hallmark of a collection is the passion of its owner, then Enid Hubbard's rabbit collection is a prime example of the genre. Her collection grew, and continues to grow; it has to, she loves it so.*

Because of their fragility and the vagaries of children, pairs of rabbits are extremely rare and difficult to find. Of the ten Mommy and Daddy couples featured, four have *Germany* or *Made in Germany* imprinted on the base. This indicates their exporters complied with American trade laws requiring identification.

Where the Easter Rabbit Came From

The rabbit, or hare, became associated with the holiday we call Easter long before the advent of Christianity. Ancient Egyptians considered the hare to be sacred; noted for its propensity to multiply, the hare was their symbol of fertility. The name Easter derives from an Anglo-Saxon rite of spring honoring Oestre, a goddess of light. In Rome, the hare, the first creature to give birth after the vernal equinox, was thought to be the personification of Minerva, the goddess of divine wisdom, or, as in the Anglo-Saxon rite, of light and life — and joyful harbinger of a vibrant spring after the deathly gloom of winter. ¶Long considered the Queen of Feasts, the pagan Easter anticipated fecundity and, ultimately, a fruitful harvest. Like the fertile hare, the egg, symbol of life, was linked to this season. The giving of eggs at the onset of spring was, in fact, a practice common to many of the world's religions, including Hindu, Islam, and Judaism. Eggs were hidden, exchanged, and eaten at their spring festivals. In Persia, eggs were colored to signify joy and to portray the vivid hues that replaced the monotones of winter. In Europe, when Easter became aligned with the Christian celebration of the Resurrection and Eternal

Life, the pagan and the sacred intermeshed. In 325 A.D., the Council of Nice officially designated the first Sunday after the first full moon of spring as Easter. ¶ In keeping with the nostalgia for a mythical or fairy-tale origin of the Easter Rabbit, one medieval story describes a princess who, wishing to express her love for her people, placed colored eggs in nests throughout her realm. Some children, reaching into a bush for a few of the eggs, encountered a rabbit there and believed him to be the bearer of these wonderful gifts. It was thought that brown eggs, or "rabbit eggs" — to distinguish them from the more common white chicken eggs — had to be colored so that they could be readily discovered in their hiding places. ¶ As the Easter Rabbit assumed greater and greater importance, his gift-giving acumen

The springtime symbols of the rabbit and the egg occasionally became so inextricably entwined that they were combined as one, either by shape — or by innuendo! The roly-poly, a familiar form, was easily adapted to a bunny-in-an-egg motif. Bunnies, by implication, birthed their young in eggs, as at left, or popped, chick-like, out of eggs, like the big bunny in the center.

A maverick among Enid Hubbard's rabbits, the 16-inch-tall farmer with alpine hat and hands in pockets glances with a bemused expression to his right through black-rimmed lithographed eyes. The words "Ungers-Cel-U-Pan Fibre Products, Unger Toy & Doll Co., Milwaukee, Wis." appear on the base, which leads to the speculation that this unknown company may have been an importer of German products in the 1920s when the rabbit was probably made. The roosters with bunnies on their backs are earlier pieces, dating from the early 1900s.

increased. Instead of seeking out hidden eggs, children expected them to be delivered, as often as not, by a rabbit garbed as a human. Eggs were typically placed in caps or baskets. By early to mid-nineteenth century, rabbit-shaped objects, with or without eggs, proliferated as a gift to celebrate the holiday. Many were designed as candy containers.

One of the ways candy manufacturers added allure to their rabbits was to paint them white and sprinkle them with very tiny glass balls, which they called Venetian dew. White, or albino, breeds of rabbit were, and are, rarer than the more commonplace browns, silvers, and greys; therefore, they were often considered more exotic or special.

How Candy Containers Evolved

In early nineteenth-century Germany (and later in England and America), when the traditional Christmas holy day began to be secularized and celebrated at home as well as in church, small fruits, nuts, and sweets were given as tokens of affection to mark the event. The gifts were not personalized. Instead they were hung all over the Christmas tree to be plucked off by adults and children alike. Because of their size, it was difficult to tie or hang the treats, so pouches of scrap fabric or netting and cones or cornucopias of paper or cardboard began to be made to hold the bounty. These were decorated with pictures, tinsel, and colored paper. ¶These containers, originally referred to as attrappen (*dummies*) or füllerartikel (*fillable articles*), were modeled on Dresdens, charming die-cut cardboard picture ornaments crafted near this German city using techniques inspired by the invention of chromolithography. Die-cutting and chromolithography made it possible to print, emboss, and cut the cardboard for decorative appeal. Dresdens were also made into three-dimensional ornaments by joining pieces together; these examples were painted and meticulously detailed to enhance their realistic allure. A sleigh, for example, would be upholstered and a horse outfitted with reins and a harness. ¶Papier-mâché took the process a step further, making it possible to mold the ornaments rather than to join flat pieces together. Molding allowed the candy containers to assume any shape the craftsperson pleased. ¶For children, candy containers doubled as toys. To please them, artisans designed containers relating to domestic life that could be turned into doll accessories; baby carriages, buckets, teacups, baskets, and hatboxes, for example, became hugely popular. ¶Children also loved containers shaped like familiar barnyard and woodland creatures. Rabbits, which, along with eggs, were symbolically connected to springtime, became the gift of choice at Easter, a holiday celebrated with the same enthusiasm as Christmas. The Oster Hase, or Easter Hare, had been introduced in 1819 in

Before World War I, a woman's place was in the home; piecework, such as painting rabbits or sewing for money, was a cottage industry and was done in a woman's "spare" time. Household tasks such as cooking and cleaning assumed greater importance. Rabbits dressed in aprons and kerchiefs emulated housewives and set a good visual example for children of the ideal *hausfrau*. Miniature stoves were advertised in early Marshall Field & Co. toy catalogs.

Sonneberg, Thuringia, then center of toy-making in Germany and the world. This first Easter Bunny was devised as a hollow toy crafted of a cheap papier-mâché mixed from brown flour paste and paper pulp. Its head was nicely designed to be removable so the

interior could be filled with candy. ¶Individual artisans or cottage craftsmen produced rabbit candy containers in their homes in tiny villages throughout Thuringia. Most families could produce between a dozen and fifteen rabbits per week. Typically, the husband would prepare the plaster mold and form the rabbit within the mold; his wife and children would paint and decorate the figures. (See pages 25 and 26 for a more detailed description of the process.) A mold did not last indefinitely. After two to four dozen rabbits

Candy containers appeal to two basic and irresistible instincts: a sweet tooth and secrets. Rabbit containers open in a variety of ways. Many realistic bunnies have twist-off heads. Others open at the waist or feet. As bunnies became ever more popular in the United States, wealthy Americans requested larger and larger containers; the uniformed figure holding a stick measures over 7 1/2 inches tall. The little girl in a bunny

had been produced, a new mold had to be copied from the old and the old discarded. When they could afford it, several families would join to purchase a variety of molds they could then share. ¶Most of the rabbits created by these individual artisans and families were realistically detailed. Several dozen breeds of rabbit proliferate in Germany; a great many containers resemble the local

chamois-colored, brown-eyed Thuringian breed. Undressed rabbits assumed three naturalistic poses: resting, sitting with their forepaws on the ground, and sitting back on their haunches. Rabbits attired in clothing stand erect, mimicking their human counterparts. ¶As rabbit containers burgeoned in popularity, especially for export to England and the United States, jobbers supplied the craftsmen with

suit, by contrast, was made before World War I. To enhance its allure, the sawdust coating the egg-shaped bunny head was sprayed with gilt. A separate cylinder inside the pre–World War I nodder on the left holds the secret cache of candy. The teeter-totter contains a primitive clockwork; like an automaton, it is set in motion by a key.

premolded figures which the artisans could paint and dress as they pleased. They were paid by the piece. Once the rabbits were completed, they were sold at markets or distributed to importers such as the American dime-store giant F. W. Woolworth and mail order companies including Chicago-based Butler Bros. and Montgomery Ward. ¶ By the 1890s, about five model makers supplied twenty-five families with materials to mold the rabbits; an additional one hundred artisans painted the rabbits and sewed the clothing used to dress them. The craftspeople

worked with matte-finish paints and with a variety of fabrics, including felt, mohair, cotton, silk, velvet, chenille, and lace. ¶ When individually hand-crafted, the rabbits retained an idiosyncratic flair. They were realistically painted, and their clothes displayed an ingenuity of tailoring and attention to detail. With the rise of cost of materials, the advent of mass production, and loss of individual artistry after World War I, the process became more mechanized. As a result, rabbits from this later period exhibited less personality.

Pussy willows, a harbinger of spring, wreathe the bunny on the large, ninety-year-old red egg on the facing page. Symbols of spring included not only the rabbit, but that eternal symbol of life, the egg. Papier-mâché eggs, decorated with chromoliths and trimmed with paper lace or embossed cardboard Dresden ornaments, were just as popular as rabbits, if not more so, as Easter gifts. Combining a bunny with eggs must have doubled the thrill for its recipient! Some Venetian dew (very tiny glass balls) still clings to the pre–World War I eggs with bunnies peeking through windows in their sides.

As soon as they were invented, motor cars and movies captured the public imagination. German manufacturers instantly responded to American requests for rabbits that would exhibit the characteristics of favorite movie personalities or types. The lop-eared rabbit controlling traffic, for instance, resembles a Keystone Cop, one early movie type that became immensely popular. The motor cars are all imaginary and do not replicate specific models.

Craft and Craftsmen

Rabbit-shaped candy containers were an outgrowth of the toy-making tradition in Thuringia. The region had long been firmly established as Germany's center for the production of porcelain. Many firms that produced porcelain tablewares expanded their range to include the manufacture of bisque heads for dolls, which were noted for their high quality. Manufacturers such as Simon and Halbig, the second largest maker, based in Gräfenhainichen, set the standard for molded porcelain and bisque and for dolls. The craft of working with papier-mâché, like bisque, relies on an expertise and dexterity in shaping molds. ¶ It takes only a short leap to imagine creating holiday candy containers that could be molded from papier-mâché to appear toy- or doll-like in form because Thuringia was also the center for the production of Christmas ornaments. Dresden was already remarkable for its embossed ornaments, which included animal shapes made from die-cut paper and cardboard. Other centers of production included the town of Lauscha, which was and continues to be noteworthy for ornaments created in glass; Neustad bei Coburg (home of the firm August Scheinorn and, later, M. Grempel); and the villages of Kronach, Ernstthal, and Litchenfels. All originally produced papier-mâché ornaments and candy containers as cottage industries, which evolved after World War I into small factories.

¶ The toy-making center of Thuringia, and Europe, was the city of Sonneberg. Between 1850 and 1860, toy manufacturer Herman Scheler became one of the first

full-time exporters of rabbit-shaped candy containers. His principal market was France, where the custom of exchanging gifts of sweets on New Year's Day had originated. An 1854 London toy bazaar and exhibition advertised Scheler's containers as "Toy Surprises," and English confectioners started importing them by the thousands. Holland followed suit a few years later. ¶ It wasn't until 1895 that candy containers finally arrived in the United States. They were first sold exclusively in bakeries and candy shops, but soon major retailers such as F. W. Woolworth and

Like motor cars, balloons and dirigibles were held in awe; miniature copies were very popular Christmas ornaments. This dirigible, fashioned of raffia and wicker like some of the cars in Enid's collection, transports a doll in a bunny suit. Rabbits with doll faces, also called snow bunnies, had bisque heads made by Thuringian manufacturers such as Simon and Halbig. Some collectors concentrate on these to the exclusion of all other types of rabbits.

Classical and folk music are integral to German culture, and so rabbits playing musical instruments were popular. Because they bear the imprint *Germany*, printed in purple, on their bases, the rabbits playing the accordion and the horn are known to have been made after World War II.

Marshall Field and the mail-order concerns of Sears Roebuck, Montgomery Ward, and Butler Bros., among others, sent representatives to Sonneberg to import the candy containers on a large scale. The rabbits remained hugely popular as long as they could be produced, but most manufacturers were wiped out during the world wars. After World War II, the New York firm of Kurt S. Adler imported small shipments to supplement their traditional holiday offerings; the firm discontinued the practice in 1955.

¶One leading manufacturer of the bunnies, Carl Schaller, founded his own company in 1894 and was able to continue working until 1941. During this half-century, Schaller hand-crafted over a hundred original molds. Schaller was one of only five mold-makers, called brossiere (one who makes molds by hand), as opposed to the twenty-five families who poured papier-mâché, and a hundred others who undertook the task of painting and dressing the figures. Most of Schaller's rabbits were sold to F. W. Woolworth, who maintained a warehouse in Sonneberg until 1939. Schaller also sold his bunnies through the large German wholesale groups of Fleischman-Cramer and Kuno-Tresel.

¶Ino Schaller, one of Carl's six sons, reopened his father's business after World War II, making figures of pressed cardboard and, by 1961, of plastic; his grandson, Dieter, made cardboard rabbits in the 1950s, trimming them with real rabbit fur, wool, and felt. Today Dieter and his son Thomas produce papier-mâché reproductions from original molds for Christopher Radko, a major importer of Christmas ornaments into the United States.

German entrepreneurs catered to America's infatuation with the circus by exporting a vast variety of rabbits costumed as clowns. The small brown and black bunny at the right, dating from the early 1900s, is the oldest in this group; all others, except for the 1930s fat fellow in the lavender suit, are from the 1920s.

Bunnies and a chuckle go hand in hand. The United States has a long tradition of satirizing its political figures in the press, so it was no great stretch of the imagination to sit President — and renowned horseman — Teddy Roosevelt upon a gigantic hare. Cartoons, too, enjoyed an enduring popularity. *The Katzenjammer Kids,* the longest-running comic strip in history (inspired by the German *Max und Moritz*), created by Rudolph Dirks, first appeared in 1897 in the "American Humorist," a Sunday supplement to the *New York Journal.* Here, a buxom Mama K. determinedly prods her charge behind Alphonse, an ultrapolite, Cyrano-nosed character drawn by Fred Opper for the Hearst-sponsored comic strip *Alphonse & Gaston.* Mama's steed resembles the local Thuringian rabbit; the "fur" boasts a yellowish cast and dark brown tips characteristic of the breed.

Working with Papier-Mâché

Papier-mâché, or "chewed paper," is, in its crudest form, a simple mixture of pulp or sheet paper and paste. Pliable when damp, papier-mâché can be easily shaped; when dry, it turns hard and strong. History books trace the origins of papier-mâché to the first century A.D. in China, where it was lacquered to make war helmets and pot lids. Gradually knowledge of the technique traveled westward into the Middle East; by 1100 A.D. the art of paper-making and papier-mâché had reached Morocco. ¶Because paper-making was a costly and time-consuming process, paper was considered a luxury until the Industrial Revolution. Individual artisans mixed up small batches of papier-mâché from recycled scrap paper that they had mashed into pulp. With the advent of machines, molds and dies were perfected to ease the process of creating objects of this accommodating material. ¶In Europe, papier-mâché first caught on as an inexpensive way to replicate architectural ornaments typically rendered in plaster. With the discovery that kaolin, a white clay used to make ceramics, could be added to the mixture, small, durable, decorative objects for the home, such as trays and boxes, as well as gifts, became enormously popular. ¶Papier-mâché candy containers originated in the southeastern region of Germany called Thuringia. Densely forested, Thuringia was home to myriad beloved creatures of folklore and fairy tales, such as elves, dwarfs, and gnomes. Not surprisingly, the region evolved into the clock- and toy-making center of Europe. It is said that the secret of papier-mâché was divulged to a toy-maker in the area by a soldier returning from

duty in the Thirty Years' War in France. French papier-mâché was renowned throughout Europe. In that country, it was fabricated into fanciful architectural embell-ishments for many of the chateaux and other municipal buildings. Because Thuringian toy-makers already relied on molding and die-cutting cardboard to make holiday ornaments, including the popular form called Dresden (see Glossary), it was natural that they adapt the

Crepe paper was invented in 1890. One of the three rabbits wearing crepe paper costumes is labeled *Made in Czechoslovakia*. This small composition rabbit with a fancy printed skirt and a bow tying its ears is the only exam-ple from that country that Enid has in her collection. From the mid-1920s until 1939, when war broke out, both Montgomery Ward and F. W. Woolworth imported rabbits from Czechoslovakia, which borders eastern Germany.

principles of papier-mâché to their repertory. The producers of papier-mâché were known as pressers. ¶It typically took a week to fabricate a rabbit from start to finish: ¶Day One: *The artisan mixed the ingredients for the papier-mâché.* ¶Day Two: *The papier-mâché was blended to a smooth consistency and then squeezed by hand into two halves of a mold formed from gypsum or from plaster of Paris. The plaster*

began to absorb the moisture from the paste-pulp mixture. ¶Day Three: *As the excess water collected in the halves of the mold, it was poured off. The remainder of the moisture slowly evaporated until the molded papier-mâché shells were completely dry.* ¶Day Four: *The dry shells were removed and dipped in a bath of liquid plaster, which formed a thin white skin over their surfaces.* ¶Days Five through Seven: *The two halves of*

Papier-mâché was embellished in a variety of ways — with mohair to simulate fur, with Venetian dew (tiny glass balls) for glitter, or with wax. A coating of wax gives the papier-mâché on this 10-inch-tall rabbit a translucent appearance. Because wax is an unstable substance that deteriorates or melts easily, few examples of the genre survive.

This pair of automata is covered with unusually curly mohair. They are large, as most automata were for adult entertainment, measuring 28 inches and 23 1/2 inches respectively. Her skirt and his alpine jacket are made of felt; this clue, as well as deep-set eyes and open keys, denote early pieces.

When this 22-inch-tall automaton is wound up, the heads of the two ducks and the head of the rabbit carrying them bob simultaneously.

the shell were joined, their seams sanded and sealed, and the shells painted. Glass eyes were set into the detachable heads. Tcuhschur, artificial fur or flocking, might be added to give a realistic fuzzy look to the rabbit. Other materials, too, were sometimes used for a textural effect; of these, cellulose shavings, mica, and tiny glass balls, called Venetian dew, were favored. The latter added sparkle to white rabbits.

Automatons, or mechanical toys, initially developed by clockmakers, were expensive to produce and were therefore designed and made for adult amusement rather than child's play. As Germany was a center of both clock- and toy-making, it is not surprising that German toy-makers produced automata as well. Many European manufacturers of mechanical figures also looked to German companies such as Simon and Halbig to supply bisque heads. Because animals were a favorite theme for toys, it is not surprising that rabbits would be made with movable parts. The wind-up key protruding from the tall gentleman rabbit on the left activates his arms and head; open keys are characteristic of automata predating 1910. Windup bunnies delivered their candies in baskets because they themselves were not hollow.

Thuringia is one of the areas of Germany thought to be populated by elves, gnomes, and other mythical for-est creatures. Rabbits posed on logs refer to a long heritage of fairy and folk tales based on forest dwellers.

Taking Care of Your Rabbits

I*t is always wise to collect rabbits that are in good condition, so examine them carefully before buying. Use your best reading glasses or a magnifying glass to inspect the rabbit, especially if the light level is low. At an auction, make a careful examination before bidding commences. If you acquire a piece that needs repair, you should consult an expert before attempting to repair it yourself. An inept repair will reduce the value of your piece and may be difficult to correct. Museums usually retain experts accomplished in different aspects of restoration; if their experts cannot help you, they usually can refer you to someone who can. If you are unsure of the type of fabric used to clothe the rabbit, for instance, an expert in textile restoration may recommend using a textile scanner to detect the age and fiber content of the fabric; the scanner may even be able to identify the climatic elements to which a fabric has been exposed. ¶For especially valuable pieces it's wise to consult an expert restorer or a museum professional even before dusting. In most cases dust can be removed with an artist's sable or camel-hair brush, a miniature hand-vacuum cleaner or a silk cloth. As a photographer,*

I can recommend a tiny blower we use to clean film. Avoid dusting with cloths made of cotton or wool; their rough texture could snag on cracks in the piece and pull off chips of paint. ¶Treasured rabbits should be kept out of direct sunlight, which causes colors to fade, especially on

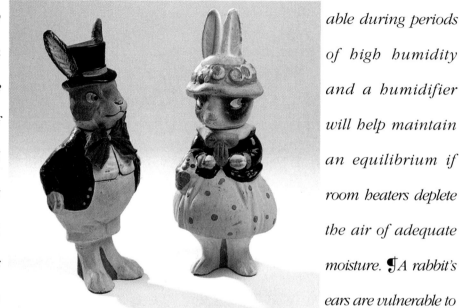

any printed paper and fabrics used to embellish the piece. Ideally the temperature in the rooms where your rabbits are displayed should hover around seventy degrees and the humidity should fall within the fifty to fifty-five percent range. If you are unsure about the volatility of the climate of your home environment, instruments are available that control temperature and humidity. Air-conditioning is extremely desirable during periods of high humidity and a humidifier will help maintain an equilibrium if room heaters deplete the air of adequate moisture. ¶A rabbit's ears are vulnerable to chips and breaks. If a bunny takes a fall, an ear might snap off. Don't attempt to refasten it unless you are sure of the proper procedure. Consult an expert restorer regarding which of the many types of glue and cement available would be best for the repair. A very fine crack may need to be touched up with paint; touch-up

Manufacturers evolved a number of ploys so that their rabbits could hold more candy. The most appealing solution was both humorous and obvious: create roly-poly, rounder rabbits! This chummy couple with removable heads — he measures 8 inches tall and she 6 inches — is attired in elegant outfits, their Easter best. The gentleman bunny boasts an oversized bow tie folded from crepe paper. A roly-poly sporting a yellow shirt opens head first to reveal its treasure trove of goodies.

painting should be done by an expert. ¶ If rabbits are to be stored, they should be wrapped loosely in acid-free tissue, placed in archival boxes, and kept in a cool, dry closet. Some archival boxes are available with partitions that make the addition of tissue unnecessary. Never wrap bunnies in plastic; plastic prevents air circulation and fabric clothing will eventually disintegrate. If your rabbit's clothing is made from wool, it is recommended you mothproof the rabbit before wrapping and boxing it. Hot attics are poor places to store valuable articles and collectibles. Few wax-covered papier-mâché bunnies have survived, because they were kept in attics where summertime heat destroyed them. Basements are also not recommended for storage, unless they are totally free of dampness.

abbits dressed in red, white, and blue, and the occasional rabbit carrying a flag, sold well. The Uncle Sam, whose head nods on a wooden pole, is 15 inches tall, the largest of the four sizes that were reproduced for export to the United States. He and the policeman ride rabbits that closely mimic the local Thuringer breed; saddles are trimmed with Dresden gold-leaf-embossed cardboard.

Because their heads bounce on coils or bob on wooden sticks, these papier-mâché rabbits are known as nodders. Springs were manufactured by machine, sticks typically carved by hand. Most nodders, though hollow, could not be filled with candy unless a separate chamber was created behind the coil or stick. Like candy containers, the earliest nodders on record date from around the middle of the nineteenth century.

It is rumored that children, both boys and girls, often helped sew clothing for the rabbits molded and painted by their parents; their work helped augment the family's income. Patterns for dolls' clothing were sold by several companies in Berlin, including H. Schubert and Winckelman & Sons, so tailored pieces such as jackets and trousers could have been sewn from such patterns. All the rabbits displayed on this antique plant stand are dressed in their original attire. Some of the clothing looks as if it were imagined; the clothing on the croquet-player, however, appears as if it might have been copied from patterns. The rabbit on the right, carrying its baby, is very early; the two date from the 1890s.

Identifying Rabbits

Although several manufacturers of candy containers have been noted and recorded, few identified their product in any way. Besides the Schaller family, other manufacturers included Fischer, Naumann; Fredrich Herold; Bucholz; Friedrich Hillman; A. C. Nestler; and Max Stopp. ¶The earliest rabbits, dating from around the end of the eighteenth century and slightly later (1807), whose papier-mâché contained flour, glue, and milk lactose, were often stored in attics and were damaged or destroyed by small animals who fed on them. Those covered with wax were damaged by heat. Others were simply discarded. These factors contribute to the scarcity of early rabbits. ¶Dating and determining the exact origin of any rabbits, early or late, present a challenge. A trained eye closely examining the materials used and the nuances of style can only make an educated guess. Although Sears, Roebuck and Montgomery Ward are known to have imported rabbits, German wholesale catalogs of the period from around 1850 to 1940 are virtually extinct except for a few in the hands of private collectors. ¶Characteristics of early rabbits include thick papier-mâché bases; heavily crinkled, stiff crepe paper; elaborate chromoliths. They were typically painted in subtle, soft tones. Many carry berries of varied sizes and thin paper flowers. They may be accented with light green Erikamoss (see Glossary). Later rabbits stand on thinner bases; crepe paper is softer and less heavily crinkled and chromoliths are simpler. If the rabbits carry berries, these are smaller and uniform in size; paper flowers are thicker. Later rabbits were painted in shiny paints in bright blues, greens, reds, oranges, purple, and pink. Accents included dark green moss and paper straw. ¶In 1893 the United States passed a law requiring all foreign imports to be labeled with their country of origin. Thus, rabbits from the turn of the century and later may have some identifying mark or name stamped on their bases. In many cases, however, the name would have been stamped on the box only; typically, the boxes were discarded. In the 1920s gummed labels were permitted. Again, because of their fragility, few remain. ¶Rabbits may be identified with the following stamps: Germany, Germany U. S. Zone, GRD, and West Germany. Some of these rabbits were made by East German artisans who found their way to West Germany after World War II, where they resumed their craft.

Adults and children alike enjoy animal toys that resemble humans in dress and habits — especially their leisure-time behavior and fancies. In the years before World War I, croquet and tennis, for example, became very popular both in Europe and in the United States. The nattily garbed croquet player sporting a green bowler stands 17 inches tall. He is an anomaly among collectibles because his maker used paints in both matte and gloss finishes; normally, matte-finish water-based paints predate enamel-based paints. The father and son tennis players may have been sold as a set. Their sweaters, which are in better condition than the trousers, were undoubtedly added later.

Scanning Enid Hubbard's desk, it becomes immediately obvious that she feels as close to her rabbits as to her family! Attention to detail marks early rabbits made by individual craftspeople who were paid by the piece. Many German papier-mâché rabbits from the 1930s were covered in cotton flannel to simulate fur; they also displayed open mouths and bright eyes made of glass. The little boy in traditional German dress astride the walking hare predates the twentieth century; his bisque head bears the mark of Simon and Halbig, a renowned manufacturer of doll heads based in Thuringia.

How to Display Your Rabbits

Displaying a collection is an art. It requires thought, study, and experimentation to create pleasing groupings with order and balance. Clustering several pieces together makes a stronger statement than spotting them around a room one by one. Pieces of lesser quality or value appear more valuable as a group than they do when they stand alone. Consider line, size, shape, color, and the texture of the pieces you are assembling. It takes practice to develop the skill of arranging individual items in a collection in pleasing compositions, but happily rabbits, sociable creatures that they are, just seem to want to be with each other. ¶ Rabbits that look well together can be assembled on chests and tabletops, organized on mantels, or collected in bookcases or in wall-hung vitrines. If your rabbits are fragile, it is a good idea to place them in a cabinet behind protective glass doors. Smaller pieces can be displayed on recessed coffee tables with glass tops or in shadowboxes designed especially for the purpose. Consider painting the background of your display in a color so that the bunnies will stand out, or install spotlights to illuminate your most precious pieces. Cabinets, open *or closed, can be equipped with special accent lighting. ¶ When placing a number of rabbits in a con-fined area, strike a balance between large and small creatures. To make sure every rabbit is visible, at least in part, position the larger rabbits in the background. If you collect same-sized rabbits in different pos-tures in one spot, it looks best to place those that are standing erect or sitting on their haunches behind rabbits in repose. ¶ Once you have created your display, do not hesitate to rearrange it from time to time, espe-cially if and when you add pieces to your collection. Study books and magazines devoted to the subject of collecting. Some recommend gathering objects by date or country of origin;*

All measuring between one and four inches in height, the rabbits standing on the 21-inch-high wooden pyramid were fabricated in the 1920s and 1930s and probably cost a penny apiece to buy at the time. Today they are rare, especially pairs such as those with removable heads in the niche at the upper left. The 3 1/2-inch-tall clown also has a head that can be removed.

A litter of rabbits runs the gamut of collectible styles — from the tiny, intricately detailed Dresden bunny in the foreground to the cartoonlike roly-poly in human garb on the left. Hard-to-find Dresdens, die-cut ornaments made of heavy paper or cardboard, are manufactured in the German city of the same name. The "eye" poking out of the back of the bunny indicates it was intended for a Christmas tree. The green rabbit is covered in flocking. Flocking, like flannel, was often used to lend texture to the papier-mâché and to simulate fur.

as you learn more about your collection, you might agree with one of these viewpoints. ¶Each room in your house will assume a distinctive "rabbit character" of its own when defined by consciously themed groupings within your collection. You might assemble rab-

bits dressed in more formal clothing in the living room, for example, while reserving those sitting on eggs or realistically posed, without clothing, for the kitchen. You can group rabbits by activity, such as pulling carts, pushing wheelbarrows, carrying flowers, or playing musical instruments, or pull them together simply by color or by texture. Your eye will tell you when you have achieved harmony. When all feels right, you will know your rabbits have indeed transformed your home and made it truly and uniquely yours.

In early times, the cornucopia, or horn of plenty, was believed to hold an endless supply of food and drink. As a symbol of abundance, the cornucopia has long been a traditional container for gifts of candy and tiny toys, especially at Christmas and at Easter. The rabbit on the right is similar to one featured at the First Easter Rabbit Museum of the World, one of a group of seven small museums in Munich where rabbits are exhibited.

Large rabbits often functioned as store displays to entice customers to browse collections of smaller containers; because they were hollow, they could have been filled with candy and sold as well. The specimen sitting in Enid's garden measures almost 22 inches in height. The straw basket straddling its shoulders would have held small gifts and samples of candy as a further inducement to make a purchase.

Until the invention of the automobile, and even after, many rural folk traveled from one destination to another by horse cart. Animals pulling carts were enormously popular with children because they could be taken apart and put together, filled and dumped. Here, a junkman rabbit leads his mates along a garden path. His seventy-year-old cart, blanketed with sponge and erikamoss, collects a medley of prized possessions: a spinning wheel, a candelabrum, and a bisque doll — and a candlelit Christmas tree. The green pig pulling the cart is said to be a symbol of good luck.

Acknowledgments

I would like to express my appreciation to the numerous individuals whose interest and encouragement made this book possible. I thank Rachel Newman, Country Living's editor-in-chief, who envisioned Enid's vast and fascinating collection as the subject of a book the moment we saw the rabbit-filled bay window on the front of the Hubbard home. Enid's generous spirit in wanting to share her beloved collection with others was essential. She credits her mother, Ruth Cloper, for teaching her to respect and care for her toys as a child. ¶ My thanks go to the Centre for Unusual Museums in Munich, Germany, for supplying information, to the staff of the Glencoe, Illinois, Public Library for their enthusiastic help, and to Robert Brenner, known especially for his authoritative books on the history of Christmas customs and decorations. The project became a special pleasure because my husband, Arthur Griggs, accompanied me on my three trips to the Hubbard home and to Wisconsin to work with Robert Brenner, and assisted me in numerous ways.

— JESSIE WALKER

Glossary

automata — spring-powered mechanical devices producing movement without continuous input from the operator. Some basic forms consist only of several pieces of cardboard producing a few simple movements. Later clockmakers created works capable of more complex movements. Many contain musical parts as well. Greeks experimented with automata as early as the third century B.C.

bisque — vitreous, hard-fired, unglazed ceramic fired only once. Although bisque is the popular term in the United States, ceramics experts say the ware should correctly be called by the French word *bisquit*.

chromolithography — a printing process employing steel embossing dies. Initially invented in England between 1820 and 1825, but perfected and used extensively in Germany throughout the century.

composition — an aggregate material formed by mixing two or more substances or ingredients.

cottage workers — artisans who work as individuals or in families in their own homes. Most materials are supplied by jobbers or manufacturers, who pay these craftspeople by the piece.

crepe paper — thin wrinkled paper resembling finely ridged or crinkled cotton or silk fabric. The indentations are more pronounced in older paper than in that of more recent origin.

die-cut paper — heavy paper that has been molded or embossed with positive and negative metal forms.

Dresden ornaments — deeply embossed die-cut heavy silver- and bronze-covered cardboard ornaments made principally in nine factories in the Dresden-Leipzig area of southeastern Germany. Three-dimensional ornaments were composed of two or more stamped pieces glued together by cottage workers. Dresdens are only two or three inches high.

erikamoss — dried bog heather indigenous to Europe. It was frequently dyed light green when used by artisans.

Foxy Grandpa — American comic strip character created by C. E. Schultz that became an immediate success when first published in 1900 in Hearst's *New York Herald*. Its popularity as a comic strip lasted only a few years but lived on as a much-used character for toys and games for nearly thirty years. Many were produced in Germany and Austria for export to the United States.

Heubach — famous German manufacturer of bisque dolls between 1820 and 1930. Gebruder Heubach or Brothers Heubach Lichte marked dolls for the export trade in English. Most are marked with an "H" in a sun over a "C."

kaolin — very fine white clay containing the mineral kaolinite, often used as a filler or extender in ceramics and refractories. It was first discovered in southeastern China.

Kewpie — doll characters created by Rose O'Neill, actress turned magazine illustrator, right after the turn of the century, when she drew pixielike Cupid characters known as Kewpies. She wrote a story about them in 1909 and in 1913 they began to be manufactured as dolls.

nodders — figures with heads mounted on springs or thin pieces of wood for movement resembling a person nodding as a greeting, a command, or a sign of drowsiness.

papier-mâché — mixture of paper pulp, starch, and glue that forms a semifirm material that is molded into shapes, and as it dries becomes hard. In the mid-1800s Frederick Muller of Sonneberg, Germany, added kaolin to the formula, increasing its strength and allowing it to be pressed easily into negative molds.

pressed cotton ornaments — unspun cotton, sometimes incorrectly called cotton wool, that has been twisted or shaped into a mold to resemble a carrot, a radish, or some other form. Glue further defines and molds the shape before it is tinted with pastel colors.

pull toys — usually an animal on a platform with wheels, pulled by either a stick or a string. Wooden animals on wheels with a string for pulling were known in ancient Egypt.

rabbit — small four-legged mammals belonging to the order of harelike animals known as *Lagomorpha*. Until fifty years ago these animals were classified as rodents, members of the order *Rodentia,* because of their burrowing and gnawing. They are found around the world.

scraps — the popular name for chromolithographs, which are full-color pictures frequently used to decorate cornucopias and papier-mâché eggs and which were sometimes applied to small Dresdens.

Simon and Halbig — The second-largest maker of doll heads in Germany, after the firm Armand Marseille, during the years papier-mâché rabbits were made. Founded in 1869 in Thuringia, Simon and Halbig produced bisque heads for themselves as well as for other companies until they went out of business in 1920.

snow babies — Dolls dressed from head to foot in a hooded, fuzzy fabric snowsuit in either pink, blue, or white, with only the face remaining visible. Some have bunny ears on their hoods.

Thuringer — A breed of rabbits accidentally produced by breeder David Gaertner in Thuringia when experimenting with Flemish Giants, Silvers, and Himalayans. The color can best be described as light reddish-yellow. A distinctive feature is the "veil" of blue-black hair tips stretching from the snout, over the cheeks, to the belly and hind quarters. The eyes are dark brown.

Venetian dew — Tiny glass balls applied with adhesive to make a piece glitter, used extensively before World War I.

waxed — Papier-mâché or composition coated with wax.

Bibliography

THIS LIST INCLUDES BOOKS ON COLLECTING, AS WELL AS FOLKLORE AND STORIES ABOUT RABBITS.
OUT-OF-PRINT BOOKS MIGHT BE FOUND IN YOUR LOCAL LIBRARY.

Aesop's Fables, retold by Ann Terry White. New York: Random House.

Arnott, Kathleen. *African Myths & Legends.* New York: Henry Z. Walck, 1963.

Brenner, Robert. *Christmas Past.* West Chester, PA: Schiffer Publishing Group, 1985.

Brown, Margaret Wise. *The Runaway Bunny.* New York: Harper & Row, 1942.

Burnett, Juanita. *A Guide to Easter Collectibles.* Paducah, KY: Collector Books, Schroeder Publishing Co., 1992.

Erdoes, Richard, transcribed and edited. *The Sound of the Flute and Other Indian Legends.* New York: Pantheon Books, 1976.

Fendelman, Helaine and Jeri Schwartz. *Official Price Guide Holiday Collectibles.* New York: Ballantine Books, 1991.

Garis, Howard Roger. *Uncle Wiggley Book.* New York: Grosset & Dunlap, 1955.

Harris, Joel Chandler. *The Complete Tales of Uncle Remus.* Boston: Houghton Mifflin, 1955.

Hertz, Louis H. *The Toy Collector.* New York: Hawthorn Books, 1976.

Hockenberry, Dee. *Collectible German Animals Value Guide, 1948-1968.* Cumberland, MD: Hobby House Press, 1990.

Horn, Maurice. *The World Encyclopedia of Comics.* New York: Chelsea House, 1976.

Jagendorf, M.A. and Virginia Weng. *The Magic Boat and Other Chinese Folk Stories.* New York: The Vanguard Press, 1980.

Johnson, George. *Christmas Ornaments, Lights & Decorations.* Paducah, KY: Collector Books, Schroeder Publishing Co., 1987.

Johnson, Lorraine. *How to Repair & Restore Practically Everything*. New York: A Mermaid Book, Viking Penguin, 1984.

Lesser, Robert. *A Celebration of Comic Art & Decoration*. New York: Hawthorn Books, 1975.

Levenstein, Mary Kerney and Cordelia Frances Biddle. *Caring for Your Cherished Posessions*. New York: Crown, 1989.

Maloney, David J. Jr. *Antiques & Collectibles Resource Directory*. Radnor, PA: Wallace-Homestead, 1994.

Pegler, Martin. *The Dictionary of Interior Design*. New York: Bonanza Books, Crown, 1978.

Potter, Beatrix. *The Tale of Peter Rabbit*. New York: Frederick Warne, 1982.

Rinker, Harry L. *Warman's Americana & Collectibles, 6th edition*. Radnor, PA: Wallace-Homestead, 1993.

Rinker, Harry L. *Warman's Antiques & Their Prices, 28th edition*. Radnor, PA: Wallace-Homestead, 1994.

Schiffer, H. N. *Collectible Rabbits*. West Chester, PA: Schiffer Publishing, 1990.

Schiffer, H. N. *Holiday Toys and Decorations*. West Chester, PA: Schiffer Publishing, 1985.

Vriends-Parent, Lucia. *The New Rabbit Handbook*. Hauppauge, NY: Barrons Educational Services, 1989.

Wells, Rosemary. *Max and Ruby's First Greek Myth*. New York: Dial Press, 1993.

Williams, Anne D. *JigSaw Puzzles*. Radnor, PA: Wallace-Homestead, 1990.